Deliciously

Victoria Parkinson

BookLeaf Publishing

Presentation by *BookLeaf Publishing*

Web: www.bookleafpub.com

E-mail: info@bookleafpub.com

ISBN: 9789357441483

First edition 2023

DEDICATION

To my sister who has recently been diagnosed with incurable cancer.

ACKNOWLEDGEMENT

To friends and family who have sippprted me through my cancer journey.

PREFACE

Writing poetry is I find a very cathartic and a great way to express feelings, emotions and experiences.

One word alone can have meaning both personal and eclectic. Then the combination of words that flow onto the next open up a world of expressionism. They can delve into deep emotional states or just be themselves in the moment. When writing poetry I am very spontaneous. Sometimes I wake up in the early hours and words appear which turn into poetry. I've sat on the bus my mind wandering and then a poem appears. The state of mind when writing poetry is one that is a blank canvas eagerly waiting to be painted. Sometimes starting in the middle or sometimes starting at the edges. Creating an image of words open to interpretation.

Time is irrelevant

Time is irrelevant time is unsure
I feel your pulse. I feel you are sure
You lift me up but I sense it's bonjour
Glance out the window through transparent glass
Seeing the vision of rain on the grass
Soaking up memories of life flashing past
One step, two step it's happening fast
I'll grab the concrete lamp post and hold to make last
Visions display the ongoing decay of virtuous array

Live life

Life live life
Live and strife
Hide and seek
Try not to peek
But go forth and speak
What you are is who you are
Who you are is how you choose
What you choose is what you desire
What you desire is what you desire
What we want is what we want
What we feel is up to us
Acceptance or cold-shoulder
Let's be bold and console
 And never be moulded into
the never ending equation

Hand in hand

Contemplating yet hesitating as I don't know
what to write
Fear not said he as he guided me on
The pressures of life go hand in hand with the
ups and downs of emotional strife
Physical feelings of torturous pain from
unknown findings as what to blame
Impassion-ate plea to flicker the flame
Let love prevail like the gorgeous sperm whale
to travel deep down to glide on the waves of our
spiritual sail

Life we have long forgotten

To the deep dark depths of sinking depression
Not wanting to feel the rising tension
No longer the wait of horrid suspension
To explore. Go forth and bravely behold the
elixir of life
Memento Vierre
Go on go on get out there
Fugit inreparabile tempus
Crack on crack on it'll soon be upon us
They say omne bonum dei donum
But what about life we have long forgotten
lost in translation whilst trapped in hesitation.
It's never to late to open the gates and wander
around without trepidation

Hold and hug

One day, this day, that day, everyday
Life does show us meaning
We live our lives and always strive to feel
emotional loving
I love you, you love me
It fills my heart with passionate meaning
To hold and hug with grounding love
The meaning of life is prolific
I'd say pro-founding but it's just astounding to
experience the onward journey.
For some it's hard to see the light that guides our
spiritual flight
We all should strive to support and guide lost
souls who fear life's beautiful calling
I love you love me
Let's open our hearts to let depart the fear of
never loving
To be as one in a changing world
Let it continue glowing

A Year

What a year, what a year, oh what a year it's been
This shit, that shit and every kinda shit
January, February Jess and Spud in heavenly beds
A few months reprive and then it starts all over again.
Me in pain I call the doctor and complain
A prod and a push I wish it was all hush hush
Sent for a scan, they then revealed the plan
Renal carcinoma I nearly fucking fell over
Kidney out I wanted to scream and shout
Pathology revealed I'm on the intensity screen,
regular scans to hopefully show I'm clean
Running alongside my wife had surgery inside
Of her legs for 3 months bed rest. We try not to feel
stressed whilst feeling blessed
having the NHS
Lots of nodules on thyroid
I hope it's nowt otherwise I'll scream and shout
Sisters in hospital 4 litres they drained.
What next to unmask
This life experiencing task
I want to confess that I'm not impressed with this shit
that shit and every kinda shit

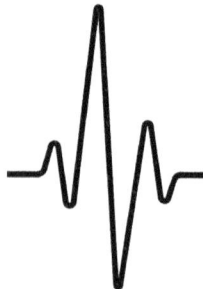

Tick-Tock

Reflecting back the light of time
Tick-tock Tick-tock
Waiting for the elusive chime
Tick-tick Tick-tock
Protruding thoughts of a none stop mind
Tick-tock Tick -tock
Irrational fears turning blind
Tick-tock Tick -tock
Two steps forwards one step back
Tick-tock Tick-tock
The hands of time are yours and mine to live our
lives and be as one
Tick-tock Tick-tock
The road is short the road is long
Searching for the eternal song
Ding-Dong Ding-dong

Intention Bound

Divine intervention of intention bound upon me
Sitting, standing turning around
Facing flashes of yonder stars
Turn to dust in those they don't trust
For fallen they are amongst baron dry lands
castles and kings
Peasants and sand
I give thee my whole supporting right hand
To pillar and prop the life that once was
I've seen them before on the standing tall cross

Poem

A poem a day keeps anxiety at bay or so they
say
The duly suppress of emotional stress brings fear
of unknown
I'm feeling alone in the tempestuous frown of
facing the facts that aren't yet back
Helpless and fractious
Happy and sad
Bring me a bag and I'll spew up the rag that's
twisting and turning
It's driving me mad!

Buying life

I went to buy some bacon in the shop the other
day
I waited for the woman 2 steps away
She paused and hesitated then ordered to
takeaway
1 pound of lamb kidneys and a fillet steak she
bought
The image of the kidney made it all so raw
It created an emotional flashback of the
surgeons healing saw
2 kidneys down to 1 and the tumour now gone
I'm sitting on a time bomb but hoping it's job
done!!

In Peace

Hate, spate spit it out
Against each other, for one another.
The searching lost souls of hatred prejudice
Answers and questions
Just let life be
Live for each other and love one another
Abundance of hate will not fumigate the
onslaught of connate.
Who you are and who we are
Lets live together in peace and calm, to flourish
and nourish
Is it all too much to ask
It's not a big task

Rising Tide

Slap, crack, almanac
The setting sun, the rising tides
To all become part of one.
Moonshine, sunshine glowing bright
The path to future earthly delights guided by
celestial sights.
Carpe omnia is the call
Free for all to bring insight
Turns the tide to personal flight

Misty Morning

Magical Misty morning high up on the hill
Vision is low but oh so full and vastly sublime
The falling leaves of time gone by surprise the
wonderous eye
Colours golden, green and brown do certainly
bring a fabulous glow
Into the earth they will descend nourish and flow
into roots below.
Protecting the creatures tiny and small
Feeding following seasonal mighty trees.
It is all but a beautiful time to nourish the mind
and settle the soul.

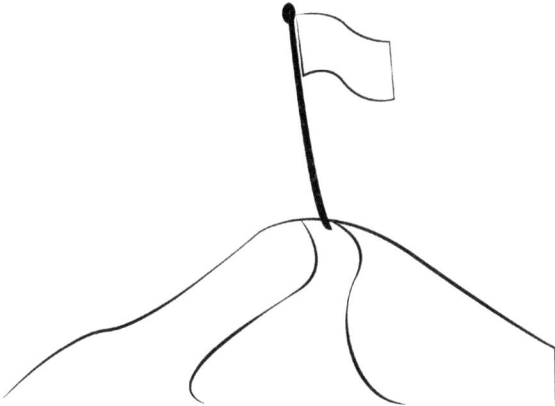

Lost Soul

Squawking starlings underneath the pier
Beach boys good vibrations playing in my ear
whilst the coast guards are searching for the lost
soul at sea

The Battles Role On

The knowledge of some is long -overdue and the
battle roles on
Do I scuttle and run
Or just grab that fucking gun
Too shoot the words that are making me numb
Day by day the nights role in and the feelings of
fear are second to none
But hear me out for I'm carrying on with my
head held high and a positive sigh

Muddles Puddles and……er

There's something about something
But I don' t know what that something is

I know that you know
But you don't know that I know

Water dripping water drop
Water dropping water drip

Splish splash splash splosh splash splish
splashing splosh

You over there I feel you are near
You over there you know I'm here
I'm over here but you're never there

What time this time
Which time every time
Time is tick tocking
Tick tocking is time

Natures Frost

Natures frost and Forrest fern
Yuletide blessings moonlight etchings
Reflecting confessing and addressing
Showing the way to a glorious day of festive
glee around the tree
The time then comes to gather up the passing
time of a year gone by
New year, new moons guide us on to future days
of shining sun
Our star that gives us life so long
In a world where everyone has a song.

Affirmations

I am free of cancer
I am free of cancer
Affirmations, confirmations, trepidations
On the ground I hear the sound so distant it is of
a hurricane wind
I get back up but get knocked down
I am free of cancer
I am free of cancer
Affirmations, confirmations, trepidations
Suzanne Vegas Solitude Standing haunts my
heart
Sister in solitude on the bed
Malignant Ascites in the blink of an eye
The emotional thug is beating me down but I'll
carry on and wear the crown
I am free of cancer
I am free of cancer
Affirmations, confirmations, trepidations

Up Down Up

Up down, down up
Up, up, up
Down down down
Not wanting to see the smiling clown
A constant reminder of fooling the sublime
A smile thats never ending penetrating the mind
Tormenting pulsating it's all a big ploy
To tempt and destroy the wandering cry

Cancer

Your a leech your a test your a twisted little
fucker
Creeping in slowly yet showing up fast
The fact of the matter too hasten the clatter of
torturous pain
Histology report seems a little to short
The cells divided can it be evaded
Betrayed or disposed I'll summon it up
That beastly disease depart from our land
We'll fight you with vigour walking hand in
hand

Water Water

Water water wash away the feelings of
impassioned decay.
Ripples forming on the tide to bring about a
peaceful ride
Swooping birds fly on by to gather up the time
to fly to migrating places
Swallows, swifts and Starlings but a few.
Murmuring songs to gather the crew.
Of you go to distant lands across the seas and
dessert sands. Bye for now and see you soon
along the tides of waters blue.

Milton Keynes UK
Ingram Content Group UK Ltd.
UKHW020752151223
434437UK00019B/902